Inspirations
A collection of modern poetry

A W Kennedy

ISBN-10: 1543208916
ISBN-13: 978-1543208917

DEDICATION

This book is dedicated to the two most special women in my life, my mother and my wife.

CONTENTS

ACKNOWLEDGMENTS

Thank you to my mother for always believing in me and pushing me to observe the world around me and the other people in it. You taught me to be tolerant and to look at things from 'their point of view'. None of my writing would have been possible without your support and encouragement.

Thank you to my wife for understanding why I have been sat at a computer for all these months working. Without your support I would not have had the time or will to complete this collection.

Many thanks to Create Space and Amazon UK for giving me the tools and support to finally make this collection a reality. Due to work and family commitments I found it very difficult to work on this project but your tools and network gave me the assistance I needed.

A pillar called life

Our life is just a pedestal,
A pillar to which we cling,
Yet, we can choose to move,
Either go up or go down,
Or we can choose to do not a thing.
Those who give up and descend down life,
Are benighted in body and mind,
Consumed by fear,
And smothered by darkness,
Ignored by the rest of mankind.
For those who descend,
Have entered a realm,
A realm of foul stench and of fear,
They call out for help,
As their pain is so great,
But so high above we can't hear.
In contrast to those who choose to descend,
Are those who try the great climb,
To rise to a platform,
Placed high above -
Mostly the meek and the kind.
I think of myself as the latter,
Attempting an open rock-face,
With only bare hands,
And strength in my heart -
No tools to pick up the pace.
To fall could prove to be fatal,
Or I could end up at the start,
That's why on the climb,
I never look down,
And try to stay strong in my heart.

Mr. Oak Tree

Big old Mr Oak tree,
Standing grand and tall,
Dominating our small park,
Overseeing all.
Standing there for years gone by,
And many years to come,
Remaining tall and strong –
Long after I have gone.
Supplying shade and shelter,
For those who come and pass,
Giving us protection,
As many years go past.
For you time moves so slow,
And for us it moves so fast,
For we are in your future,
And you are in our past.
You hardly seem to notice,
As I sit here and stare,
Underneath your canopy,
I doubt you even care!
As everyday I see you,
I envy you in a way,
You're so grand and carefree,
No worries in your way.
As you grow older, As do I,
And I pass you by each day,
Yet I get weak, as you grow strong,
Heading skyward all the way.
So goodbye Mr Oak tree,
I may be gone someday,
Maybe a child of mine will pass,
And say hello someday.

My Dearest Marie

My Dearest Marie,
You're everything to me,
My first thought in the morning light,
And my last thought at night.

You're like no one I've ever met before,
I want to be with you more and more,
I'd gladly give up everything for you,
Just to be with you.

It's like I've known you all my life,
One day I hope you'll be my wife,
I can see a future with you forming,
A new chapter in our lives dawning.

It's so exciting with you making plans,
As I know they can come true,
We'll help each other through it all,
You there for me – and I for you.

There'll be big changes in our lives,
As we venture on grounds anew,
Hopefully many good times follow,
And bad times will be few.

I want to be with you forever,
To live happily ever after,
To spend our lives together,
In joyfulness and laughter

Teenage Life

Life is Fine, Fun and Sweet,
Fine and fun when friends you meet,
Sweet in food and spice of dare,
But to some, like me –
Lift is but nightmares.
Constant danger, looking back,
No piece of time when to relax.
Mugging is accepted – nothing new to me,
It's part of the world we live in,
Part of society.
People always shouting,
Children yelling too,
No apparent reason, nothing really new.
So is life fine, fun and sweet?
Not to me or friends I meet,
Life is rough, unfair and bitter,
But in a world like this –
To whom does it matter?

A Devils Claw

In the darkness rain beat down,
Pounding on my weary crown,
I thought about my small cabin,
And all the warmth contained within.
As I walked along the street,
I spied an object near my feet,
As I bent down to examine more,
It looked like twas a devils claw;
As I grasped it in my hand,
A quiet rumble crossed the land,
The sound became a mighty roar -
A voice called out :
" Your faith no more "
The devil rose up from the ground,
As lightening cracked and boomed around,
The devil let a fearsome roar :
" Give me back my other claw "
The devil sneered,
" I'll take your soul ;
Till be like all the days of olde,
It shall be as it was before -
But I must have my other claw !"
I dropped the claw onto the floor,
The devil hissed:
" Your faith no more "
I grasped a lantern from the wall,
I threw it at the devil tall,
The flames consumed him one and all .
The devil was no more.
And still when nights,
Are cold and dreary,
And I sit so warm and weary,
 I sit and watch my devils claw,
 Which now hangs on my cabin wall,
 I hear a voice : *" Your faith no more "*

Nieces Causing Trouble

Naughty little rugrats,
Into everything they see,
Everything so new and different,
Cute when they want to be.
Everyday a new adventure,
Something new to do,

Causing havoc in the park -
And smelly nappies too!
Understanding most things,
Shouting for their mom,
In and out under your feet,
Nothing much gets done.
Getting up to mischief,

Trampling down the flowers,
Running all around the garden -
Out for at least two hours.
Up the apples and pears -
Bout time you went to bed,
Lay down in-between the covers,
Eyes closed, now rest your head.

User friendly?

Eventually, at last,
My brand new PC,
Will soon be up and running,
Easy as can be.
Monitor,
Keyboard,
Computer House,
And this little thing -
Must be the mouse.
Windows something,
And what is DOS?
Now I am confused,
Now I'm at a loss.
Why isn't it working?
What haven't I done?
Trust me to buy one,
That has to go wrong.
Where does this plug go?
And what do I press?
So much for user friendly,
I'm in a right mess!
So much for the manual,
And the disk which fell out,
Three point what? Disk protection?
What's it all about?
I'd better 'phone the shop up,
They'll know what has to be done,
And maybe they can tell me,
How to turn the damn thing on!

Gulf Conflict 1991

The sun burns my face,
As its reflected from the sand,
The light hurts my eyes and to see I raise my hand.
The desert smoothed out,
Like a calm, golden ocean,
Only rarely disturbed by a soldier in motion.
Dug in like animals in their shallow fox-holes,
They watch through their gun-sights for Iraqi patrols.
All military transport camouflaged for protection and placed under netting
to prevent their detection.
All tank tracks have loosened because of the sand,
They need to be tightened –
This is done so – by hand.
All men are alert and ready to fight,
To defend small Kuwait,
Against Iraq's might.

Dedicated to all Soldiers who served in the Gulf War

Lost ones

Loss is very painful,
Not for those that go,
But for the loved ones left behind,
Who's hearts are full of woe.
When you lose a loved one,
A loved one very kind,
They may go in the physical,
But they live on in your mind.
A loved never really goes,
As their memory lives on,
They'll never be forgotten,
Their spirit still lives on.
Their spirit will be in their children,
And the work they did each day,
So any loved one who may have left,
Is still with us today.

Butterflies

Beautiful the butterflies,
As they flutter and prance,
About the English countryside,
In their own majestic dance.
I sit among my garden,
And a Comma flutters o'er,
Its lands but a yard away,
Balanced on a flower.
No-more colours have I seen,
Than upon the insects back,
Startling red and emerald green,
Set on a sheet of black.
Red admirals, White admirals,
Peacocks I adore!
Some of the many species,
That I cannot ignore.
These so beautiful creatures,
Bring colour to my mind,
I only wish their being here,
Was for a longer time.

Don't Leave Us

It nearly took you from us,
We've tried to make you stay,
We always want you with us,
But we're living for today.
Although we nearly lost you,
And our hearts broke at the thought,
We think of all the love we've shared,
And the happiness you've brought.
Now it's only a matter of time,
A waiting game we play,
We love you all we can each day,
And hope it stays that way.
You brush your head against my hand,
As if to say you know,
That we did everything that we could,
To never let you go.
You'll always be remembered,
We've shared our lives as one,
My tears fall as I write this,
I'll miss you when you're gone.

I Think Of You

I think of you,
And a smile creeps across my face,
My minds starts to drift away,
My thoughts in outer-space.
I only hear the music,
As we dance arm in arm,
Embracing each other -
Free from all harm.
Your hair against my face,
Your warm chest against mine,
As we sway to the music,
Forgetting about time.
Each other exploring,
Roaming hands on the dance floor,
It's time we were leaving,
For I'd like to do more.
Then I wake with a blush,
As my colleague gives a shout,
I've been thinking of you again,
Of that there's no doubt.
I'll see you again,
When I next think of you,
Then we can do all the things,
That our bodies long to do.

For Sonia

On that day the rain beat down,
Echoing the tears of all around,
For the skies grew dark,
As we began to pray,
As our dear friend Sonia,
Was leaving that day.
Bubbly and young,
You lit up the room,
A bright ray of sun shine,
To pierce the gloom.
Always fresh and beautiful,
Taking life in your stride,
You'll never be forgotten,
Dear Sonia, full of pride.
Many hearts were broken,
As we said goodbye that day,
We try to understand,
Why you had to go away.
You'll never be forgotten,
For in our lives, you've left a space,
And a picture in our memories,
Of your cheerful smiling face.

In memory of Sonia Flight who left us too soon.

An Old Man

I saw an old man,
As he flew through the air,
With a pipe in his mouth,
And the wind in his hair.
I was surprised,
'Cause the man flew quite far,
But he wasn't happy,
He was hit by a car.
At the end of his flight,
The old man was alive,
It was the car backing up,
He didn't survive!
A lesson to all,
When crossing the street
To look left and then right,
And be quick on your feet!

An Old Woman

I met an old woman,
With brown, greying hair,
And dark yellow dentures,
And an icy cold stare.
She worked in a cake shop,
In Scotland, near Fife,
She put me off cakes,
For the rest of my life!
She used her false teeth,
To edge off the pies,
And made holes in the doughnuts,
With her dark brown glass eye!

Best Gift Of All

The nights were long and the days cold,
We kept warm inside,
We cuddled closely in the chair,
With you close by my side.

I think of Christmas years ago,
As the day came to a close,
As I held your hand in mine,
And decided to propose.

As you said yes and wore my ring,
No happier could i be,
I had the greatest gift of all -
My fiancé here with me.

Now every Christmas morning,
With the presents under the tree,
I awake with the best gift of all,
With my wife next to me.

Dedicated to my wife Marie

The Silence

In the car on the way home,
The silence thick and heavy,
Weighs a ton upon his mind,
As they drive on - silent, steady.
They rarely speak when they're alone -
A tragedy to know,
A son and father cannot talk,
'Cause the barriers aren't that low.
He racks his brains for things to say,
But nothing comes to mind,
And so the silence stretches on,
Dead, uncomfortable, unkind.
And so when they finally stop -
He jumps out with a gasp,
Able to leave the dreadful silence,
And breathe again at last.
He hopes one day,
The barriers fall,
And the silence is filled with laughter,
Then they can be father and son,
And live from there on after.

To Go

It was time I left,
I had to go,
It's going to be difficult,
For all – I know.
I couldn't take this world –
I couldn't take the pain,
I didn't want to wake up again.
I didn't mean to hurt you all,
I just wanted to be at rest,
You all know the problems I've had,
I thought it's for the best.
Don't be sad – don't cry for me,
I had planned this for a while,
I want to join my long gone friends,
To see them again and smile.
Please don't be angry,
Remember me as you do,
Don't remember me leaving this way,
I always am with you.
I wish that I could've said goodbye,
In a better way,
I didn't want to leave a note –
But I saw no other way.
I hope in time you'll understand,
I had to go today,
I don't feel any pain now,
That's why I couldn't stay.

ABOUT THE AUTHOR

A W Kennedy grew up in the West Midlands and started writing in his early teens. He has a love of nature and animals and a respect for the natural world which shows in much of his work. Through poetry competitions and magazines he was published regularly until he took a break from writing to relocate to start a new life on the edge of the New Forest. In this selection of poems you can see some of the inspirations that influenced their creation - the political to the personal, the love to the sorrow.